But God Said...

A Mother and Son's Courageous Journey to a New Heart

Markel Crockton
Liz Crockton

Copyright © 2022 by Markel Crockton and Liz Crockton

Edited by Regina A. Byrom

All rights reserved. No part of this book may be reproduced, stored in a retrieval system, or transmitted in any form by any means electronic, mechanical, photocopying, recording or otherwise without written permission of the publisher, except for the inclusion of brief quotations in a review.

Unless otherwise indicated, Scripture quotations taken from the King James Version (KJV) – public domain.

BUT GOD SAID: A MOTHER AND SON'S COURAGEOUS JOURNEY TO A NEW HEART/MARKEL CROCKTON AND LIZ CROCKTON – 1ST Edition

ISBN: 9798986397573
First Printing, October 2022
Printed in the United States of America

Publishing Services Provided by:
STePH Publishing, LLC
Waldorf, MD

Acknowledgements

First of all, I would like to thank God for answering my prayers, healing my body, and giving me a second chance at life.

I am grateful and thankful to my unknown organ donor and to his family for providing me with his heart that beats in my chest.

I would like to thank my mother for her unwavering faith, love, prayers, and support. Equally, I thank her for encouraging me to share my story by authoring this little book with her as a platform to share about the power of God, the power of His Word, the power of His grace, and the gift of healing.

Thanks to my two daughters, Marnier and Lauren, who were my inspiration to fight and live. Thanks to them for staying focus and on task in school when I know it was not easy. And a big thanks to them for starting a nonprofit organization, Daddy's Big Heart Fund, on my behalf.

Thanks to my family and friends for just being there for me, my mother, and girls. I am thankful for your unconditional love, prayers, monetary gifts, fund raisers, and visits that made some of my darkest moments brighter.

I thank God for my team of cardiac doctors, surgeons, nursing staff, and all those who managed my care over the years at Brigham and Women Hospital in Boston. They were some of the most kind and supportive people in their field.

I thank my church family, especially my pastors, at Twelfth Baptist Church, in Boston. I am thankful for a church of prayer that warred and petitioned heaven on my behalf.

Last but not least, I thank Stephanie Carter's STePH Publishing, LLC for helping us through the process of publishing our first book, "But God Said." We look forward to partnering with her on more projects in the future.

-Markel Crockton

Foreword

"And whatever you ask in prayer, you will receive, if you have faith" (Matthew 21:22).

I had the awesome privilege of meeting Minister Liz Crockton through a mutual friend, Glynnette Byrom Scott. I knew from our first conversation that she was going to change my life…and she has. I knew immediately that I was speaking with a woman of incredible faith and endurance, and I knew this before I read about her son's remarkable journey to receive a new heart.

When I started reading the manuscript of *"But God Said…,"* I could not put it down. It took me on an emotional rollercoaster. Her description of spending nights in the hospital, seeing her son in tremendous pain, discovering that the hospital lost part of his skull, and the countless surgeries to keep Markel alive, became very personal to me being the mother of two sons. *"But God Said…"* is a testament of what they went through and it springs forth her love for God and her love for her son. Her journey has inspired me in so many ways, and I am blessed to have such a woman of faith and prayer in my life. She calls me a "daughter" since Markel and I are the same age. Minister Liz and Markel Crockton's testimony spotlights the unconditional love that God has for us and how He never leaves us nor forsakes us during life's trials and troubles.

I am honored to have worked with Minister Liz and Markel on publishing their remarkable story. I am blessed that our paths have crossed, and I know that you will be blessed, too.

Stephanie D. Carter
Founder and President
STePH Publishing, LLC

Foreword

"For we walk by faith not by sight." II Corinthians 5:7

Elizabeth Crockton, an incredibly phenomenal woman, has dedicated her life to service and impacting the lives of so many who have entered her life. She, herself, would be challenged as she travails through the most traumatic experience of her life. As a water-walker, her faith is unwavering, when it comes to praying for her son and herself through this life-changing experience. Her faith is an example to others, as we go through the vicissitudes of life, knowing that our God is with us.

I personally witnessed her strength each time I entered the hospital room of her son, she could be found sitting there (sometimes standing), just her and her God communing and strategizing next steps for the undeniable miracle that would occur. For over a series of years, Elizabeth camped out and created a comfortable second home for herself as she and the angels stood watch over her son.

A mother's love never stops, no matter the circumstances. This I saw in my friend and mentor, as she reaffirmed the true meaning of unconditional love and unshakable faith. No matter how grim the report, she believed in her God. No matter the fierce attacks of the enemy, she believed in her God, no matter the incomprehensible circumstance's she believed in the impossible: He who specializes in things that seem impossible, her God.

From the beginning to the end of this ordeal, she believed, and her faith brought her and Markel through. Read how she captures the experience and how she pulls you into her pain, her indecision, her joy, her peace, her steadfastness, and her triumph. This was definitely a faith walk, and my sister mother, walked right through, standing on the Word of God.

Once you pick up "But God Said…," you will not be able to put this book down until the very last page.

Elizabeth and Markel are passionate writers, who brilliantly paint the vibrant canvas as they thread words together, captivating their audience. Each one brings you into the hospital room, into their frailties, in their prayers, and into the Word of God that is weaved throughout this book. You will find solace. Through their literary genius, I look forward to reading many more pieces of their work.

Donette l. Wilson-Wood

Minister, Educator, Motivational Speaker, Writer, and Mother

Table of Contents

Acknowledgements .... *i*
Foreword by Stephanie D. Carter .... *ii*
Foreword by Donette I. Wilson-Wood .... *iii*

Part I - My Journey

Introduction *1*
Chapter 1 Knock-Knock *5*
Chapter 2 The Story Behind My Testimonies *14*
    Testimony # 1 .... *14*
    Testimony #2 .... *16*
    Testimony #3 .... *19*
    Testimony #4 .... *21*
    Testimony #5 .... *23*

Part II - From My Mother's Journal About My Journey

Introduction *24*
My Son's Journey: 2010 Journal Entries *26*
My Son's Journey: 2011 Journal Entries *28*
My Son's Journey: 2012 Journal Entries *34*
My Son's Journey: 2013 Journal Entries *38*
My Son's Journey: 2014 Journal Entries *44*
Conclusion *60*
Call to Action *62*

But God Said...

A Mother and Son's Courageous Journey to a New Heart

PART I

MY JOURNEY

Introduction

"The life of faith is not a life of mounting up with wings, but a life of walking and not fainting...Faith never knows where it is being led, but it loves and knows the One who is leading." – Oswald Chambers

If we live long enough, trials and tribulations will knock at the doors of our lives to test our faith. It will not matter if we are saved or unsaved, young, or old. At some point, we will have to respond to those tests and knocks. My faith was tested over a course of 10 years when an unexpected diagnosis came knocking at my door. Every major organ in my body… my heart, brain, lungs, and kidneys were attacked by the evil one. Why the test? Why the attacks? I did not know, but I can testify that God gave me strength to push beyond the initial shock and fears that flooded my soul. Upon hearing the news of my condition, prayer warriors from all over the country started warring and petitioning God on my behalf through prayer.

None of us knows how we will respond when misfortunes come. For me, I had to fight in the arena of faith with my eyes fixed on Jesus. I had to seek God, pray, stand, and pull on the Word of God…believing He would never leave me to fight alone.

In the end, I witnessed God making the impossible become possible and the unknown known to me.

Getting to healing and wholeness was a process. I had to learn how to grow my faith. I had to learn how to get into His presence, through prayer, and reading His word for revelation. Before my health diagnosis, I went to church, was saved, served on ministries, but lacked a deeper relationship with God.

Once I learned how to get into His presence, things began to turn around for me. He revealed Himself as my trusted friend, my healer, and my deliverer. In prayer, He would speak. He revealed not to look at my current circumstances; nor be deceived by what my natural eyes would behold, or what my ears would hear, but to keep my eyes focused on Him...Jehovah Rapha, "The Lord who heals you."

As you read each page, you will witness the grace and mercy of God on my journey of healing and restoration.

I am sharing my testimony of faith to bear witness to the unlimited power and mercy of God that is also available to you. I never thought I had a testimony worthy of sharing. I thought testifying was something old folks did, but after going through a series of storms in my life, I knew it was God who was shielding and keeping me safe and secure. I refused to allow the devil or my insecurities to hold my testimony captive, especially if my testimony can give hope to someone. Revelation 12:11 says, *"And they overcame him by the blood of the Lamb, and by the word of their testimony."*

My testimony is that God healed me in spite of my health prognosis. He rescued me from the grips of the evil one. He restored my health.

Professor Alex Bradford wrote a song which states: *"I said I wasn't going to tell nobody, but I couldn't keep it to myself, what the Lord has done for me."*

We have evidence in the Bible..."When Jesus healed the sick and raised the dead, they ran and told what God had done for them. When the blind man received sight, he went and told others. When the Samaritan woman received living water from Jesus, she could not wait to tell others what Jesus had done for her." I too am coming forth to tell my story about the healing hands of God that saved and spared my life. Hallelujah!

I hope the testimonies in this book will give you hope about the power of God, to seek his face, and believe in Him. There is a song by Stuart Hamblen that says, *"It is no secret to what God can do, what He's done for others, He will do for you."* God will never leave you nor forsake you in your hour of need. God is able. Hold on to the fact that God can do what no other power can do. He tells us in Deuteronomy 31:6 (KJV) *"Be strong and of good courage, fear not, nor be afraid of them: for the LORD, thy God; he will not fail thee, nor forsake thee."* This is a beautiful promise to take hold of.

God is always faithful to fulfill that which He has said in His Word.

2 Corinthians 1:20 KJV says, *"For all the promises of God in him are yes, and in him Amen, unto the glory of God by us."* What a gift from God in this promise!

I can testify that if you are going through a trial or have been given life-changing news that is getting ready to carry you into a storm, stand on God's Word which says in Psalm 107:29, *"He maketh the storm a calm, so that the waves thereof are still."* Believe that God can cease the storms from raging in your life. But when storms rage:

- Grab hold to God's unchanging hand and let nothing pull you away from His grip

- Stand on His word and promises for your life.

- Solicit a band of prayer warriors who believe in the power of prayer and will go to war for you.

- Keep the faith and encourage yourself, especially when *your current situation does not mirror God's promises for your life.*

It is my prayer that my story of God's grace will give you hope and strength for your journey if you are facing raging storms in life.

I am thankful to my mother for being obedient to God by keeping a prayer journal and capturing parts of my journey over the years. I could see the wonder-working power of God's mercy and grace in each stage of my journey through her journal.

I am blessed that God gave me a mother who is a prayer warrior, obedient, faithful, and listens to Him by following His will and way. She never gave up on God for my healing here on earth, even when her faith was tested. She just unlocked the resources of heaven by standing on His promises and being steadfast in prayer for my life.

- **Markel Crockton**

> "I refuse to allow the devil or my insecurities to hold my testimony captive, especially if it can give you hope to fight with courage any raging storm you are facing in your life."
>
> -
>
> *Markel Crockton*

CHAPTER 1
Knock-Knock

Jesus said, "in this world, you will have tribulation: but be of good cheer"
(John 16:33b KJV).

Life is not a joke. As children, we often played pranks on each other or just had fun telling jokes and laughing. Growing up, our family loved playing Knock Knock Jokes. In those jokes, we would come up with some clever name that sounded like another name to keep one guessing. For example, we might say, "Orange." We would ask, "Orange who?" The one doing the knocking would come up with the last name that was funny or unique to make everyone laugh or say, "That is a corny joke." … "Orange you happy?"

Childhood Knock Knock jokes were meant to be funny, but what about the "knocks" that come at the doors of our life that are not jokes. The knocks when we ask, "Who is there?" and the response is "Trials and tribulation." "Trials and Tribulation who?" Trials to test your faith and trust in God. Tribulations that bring pain, distress, and sickness. We will say, "Stop joking, this is not funny." Their knocking, however, does not cease.

Our first inclination is to try and ignore the knocking, thinking it will stop, but the knocking just gets louder and more intense. Then, we realize that there are some knocks that we cannot stop. Our effort is pointless. We call upon Jesus, who says, *"I am the door"* (John 10:9a) to answer the knocks and help us.

Have you ever had one of those unexpected knocks in your life that changed the trajectory of your life?

I can attest that knocks come at the door of our lives to test the depth of our faith and trust in God. It will not matter if we are saved or unsaved, a billionaire or a "penninaire," happy or sad, young, or old, educated, or uneducated… something or someone will come knocking.

One of the loudest, continuous knocks I encountered came from trials and tribulation. I had to ask, "What are you doing here?" Tribulation said, "You will have to endure some significant suffering and pain." I asked, "Why?" "A virus has attacked your heart, and now you have cardiomyopathy. Over the years, your heart will get weaker, and you will need a heart transplant to survive," said Tribulation. "This cannot be true," I said. "I am young, healthy, and fit."

Trials said, "Your faith will be tested and stretched to the limits. Storms will come and will keep on raging in your life for seasons. Faith said, "When you are going through storms, remember God is in the storm with you keeping watch over you, shielding you, and protecting you. So, keep your eyes fixed on Jesus."

The devil with his cohorts, doubt, and fear, came knocking: "How many people do you know have had a heart transplant? How many years does one wait to get a heart? Most people die waiting. Did you know that?"

With help from my mother, I used the words of God to combat every contrary notion that Satan tried to throw my way.

I said, *"Away from me, Satan!"* (Matthew 4:10b KJV). *God has given me a spirit not of fear but of power, love, and self-control" (2 Timothy 1:7).* And God's Word, *"shall not return unto me void, but it shall accomplish that which I please, and it shall prosper in the things whereto He sent it" (Isaiah 55:11).*

The devil kept trying to spread doubt in my mind, but the Spirit kept whispering, "Have faith, and trust in God's Word."

The devil came knocking again in a different season saying, "With your condition, you could die young." But The Word says, *"With long life will I satisfy him and show him my salvation" (Psalm* 91:16).

The devil said, "You will be defeated. You will not win this health fight." I stood on the Word saying, *"We are more than conquerors through Him that loves us" (*Romans 8:37 KJV).

The devil tried to scare me with worry, "You will lose all your earthly wealth, savings, job, health insurance, houses, cars, and friends." However, I stood on the Word, *"Be strong and of good courage; be not afraid, neither be thou dismayed; for the Lord, thy God is with thee"* (Joshua 1:9b). *"Beloved, I wish above all things that thou mayest prosper and be in health, even as thy soul prospereth"* (3 John 2 KJV). *"Shall we accept good from God, and not troubles?"* (Job 2:10)

The devil came gloating, "God is the One putting you through these trials and tribulations. Don't you go to church, tithe, pray, and worship Him?" But I said, *"For a certainty, God does not act wickedly, the Almighty does not pervert justice"* (Job 34:12 NIV). And *"I will bless the Lord at all times: his praises shall continually be in my mouth. My soul shall make her boast in the Lord"* (Psalm 34:1-2b NIV).

The devil tried to attack my thoughts and mind, but the Spirit of God stepped in and said to me, "Do not amplify the devil's evil doing and minimize My power. Do not entertain him. I have everything in control. I am bigger and more powerful than your storms or anything he throws at you. In fact, I am the same God who calmed the storm on the Sea of Galilee when My disciples became afraid (Mark 4:35-41). Keep trusting Me and guard your mind. Stand on my Word and *"Cast down imaginations, and every high thing that exalteth itself against the knowledge of God and bringing into captivity every thought to the obedience of Christ"* (II Corinthians 10:5 KJV), and *resist the devil, and he will flee from you"* (James 4:7 KJV).

Our Mind

I know that our mind is a precious gift from God that stores our testimony and houses our faith in God. Think about it. If the devil can control our mind, he can whisper all kinds of misleading falsehoods hoping to plant fear, evil thoughts, and doubt. His goal is to make you think that God has abandoned you, and all your friends have forsaken you. Ultimately, He wants to destroy our relationship with God and eventually destroy our life.

Combat his lies by pulling on the Word of God to expose him for who Jesus says he is - *"The father of all lies"* (John 8:44 KJV). What kinds of lies have the devil tried to tell you concerning your circumstances, health, or healing contrary to the Word of God? Do not fall for his lies. The Word tells us to, *"Set our affection on things above, not on things on the Earth"* (Colossians 3:2 KJV).

Pray that God will strengthen your faith where it is weak and fill your mind with hope as you wait on Him for your breakthrough and healing.

Praying the Word

It is impossible to go through trials and come out on the other side whole without putting a demand on God's Word. He tells us what we can have through His word. As long as you know what His Word says, then anything promised to us in His Word is always His will for us.

Praying God's Word and promises over our situation is serious business for our deliverance and healing.

The Bible says in John 15:7, *"If you abide in Me, and My Word abide in you, you will ask what you desire, and it shall be done for you."*

Deeper Revelations Through Scriptures

The Spirit of God continued speaking and ministering to my spirit through His word.

First, His Word said, *"When you pass through the waters, I will be with you; and when you pass through the rivers, they will not sweep over you. When you walk through the fire, you will not be burned; the flames will not set you ablaze"* (Isaiah 43:2 NIV).

What a powerful assurance of God's protective grace. This Scripture gave me peace of mind that God is on this journey with me. He is with me in trials, pain, suffering, and the raging storms. God is the One keeping me from being consumed or set ablaze from the trials of life. Lamentations 3:22-23 KJV states, *"It is of the Lord's mercies that we are not consumed, because his compassions fail not. They are new every morning: great is Thy faithfulness."*

Second, God reminded me to stand in the arena of faith through trials. Why? Because His Word says, *"But without faith it is impossible to please him: for he, that cometh to God must believe that he is and that he is a rewarder of them that diligently seek him"* (Hebrews 11:6 KJV).

I have found that the word faith is difficult to explain by reason or logic. But the Word in 1 Timothy:6a says, *"Fight the good fight of faith."*

In Hebrews 11:1 (KJV), it says, *"Now faith is confidence in what we hope for and assurance about what we do not see."*

Faith defies logic and goes beyond just hoping. Beyond hope implies that something is dire and cannot be fixed. But thank God for faith. Faith says, you know, that you know in your heart and soul, that everything will be all right.

Third, *God's Word revealed: "Do not be afraid or discouraged because of this vast army. For the battle is not yours, but God's"* (2 Chronicles 20:15b NIV). There are just some things we are not equipped to handle without God's divine intervention. My health fight lasted for over ten years. There were times when I did become fearful and discouraged. I knew I was in a battle–a battle to steal my health, faith, and to beat me down. But I knew that God was bigger than any battle in my life. The battle was His to reveal His power and might and let me know that no one can battle with the Almighty and win. The good news is…my God fought my battle and allowed me to enjoy the victory.

The fourth revelation, *"No temptation has overtaken you except what is common to mankind. And God is faithful; he will not let you be tempted beyond what you can bear. But when you are tempted, he will also provide a way out so that you can endure it"* (1 Corinthians 10:13 NIV). I know God would not place no more on me than I could endure. My way out was through His Promise that says, *"Call on me in the days of trouble; I will deliver you, and you will honor me"* (Psalm 50:15 NIV). I stood on this promise and called on Jesus for deliverance.

The fifth revelation was Psalm 121. This Psalm wraps my soul in the goodness of what God can do. It is comforting to know that my God is my keeper, my help, watches over me, protect me from harm, and will preserve my soul.

I prayed these words over my life: *"I will lift my eyes unto the hills, from whence cometh my help. My help cometh from the Lord, which made heaven and earth. He will not suffer thy foot to be moved: he that keepeth thee will not slumber. Behold, he that keepeth Israel shall neither slumber nor sleep. The Lord is thy keeper: the Lord is thy shade upon thy right hand. The sun shall not smite thee by day, nor the moon by night. The Lord shall preserve thee from all evil: he shall preserve thy soul. The Lord shall preserve thy going out and thy coming in from this time forth, and even for evermore"* (Psalm 121 KJV).

As I continued to meditate upon God's Word, wonders started happening:

- I received spiritual revelation, insight, and assurance that I was going to be all right. I did not know how or when, but I knew everything was going to work out in my favor.

- I found peace of mind in the midst of pain and suffering.
- I received strength to keep moving…one step at a time…one day at a time.
- I felt the power of God ministering to the birthplace of my needs.
- His Word became spiritual food that fueled and nourished my soul as I looked to heaven daily, lingering there in prayer, and pouring out from the depth of my soul to God.

As I prayed, this Psalm took on a new meaning to me:

I prayed: Father God, Your goodness is not withheld from me. Like David, I too can look unto the hills from which cometh my help. I affirm that my help cometh from You. Healing cometh from You. Blessings cometh down from You. And every good and perfect gift cometh down from above.

Father God, I come to Your mercy seat, pleading for healing, here on earth. I am standing on Your Word and Promises, knowing your word will not return void but will perform that which you declared. Your Word tells me that you will keep me from all evil. Even if I must walk through the valley of the shadow of death, I will fear no evil; for you are with me.

Father God, you are my keeper and protector from all dangers seen and unseen. You hold my feet steady on the shaky ground. You never slumber nor sleep. Your eyes are always upon me, wiping away my tears, and attending to my pain and every need. Your Word says, "Your eyes are on the righteous, and Your ears are attentive to their prayers." I bless Your name.

Father God, hear my prayer as I stand bare before You. I know You do all things well. I surrender my will for Your will to be done in my life. I bless Your Holy Name as I look unto the hills from which cometh my help. In Jesus' Name, I pray, Amen.

Warning Scriptures

In some of the darkest moments of my life, the Word of God prepared me to identify what and who I was fighting; who was out to destroy me; and what I needed to do to become an overcomer through Christ Jesus.

The Word of God revealed

First in Ephesians 6:11-12, The Word told me I was fighting against unnatural forces... rulers of the darkness of this world; principalities; and spiritual wickedness in high places. But the good news is, God has provided me with spiritual weapons to fight the fiery darts of the devil.

First, God provides spiritual armors of protection that I had to wear in this fight:

The Belt of Truth

The Breastplate of Righteousness

The Gospel of Peace

The Shield of Faith

The Helmet of Salvation

The Sword of the Spirit- Word of God

And Prayer

Second, He equipped me with Spiritual weapons for battle:

Pleading the blood of Jesus

Calling on the Name of Jesus

Praying the Word of God

Reading God's Word

Worshiping and Praising God

Walking in Faith

My Testimony of faith

The truth is, *"We wrestle not against flesh and blood, but against principalities, against the rulers of the darkness of this world, against spiritual wickedness in high places. Therefore, we should put on the whole armor of God and take every spiritual weapon in our possession to fight and stand against the fiery darts of the devil"* (Ephesians 6:11-12).

- *The Word also warned me that," The thief comes to steal, and to kill, and to destroy. I have come that they may have life and that they may have it more abundantly"* (John 10:10 NIV).

- *And this Word said, "Be sober, be vigilant; because your adversary, the devil, as a roaring lion, walketh about, seeking whom he may devour"* (I Peter 5:8 KJV).

God does warn His children through His Word to keep us from being spiritual stranded when trials come.

Father God, You has allowed me to survive too many STORMS to be bothered by a few RAINDROPS!

-

Anonymous

CHAPTER 2

The Story Behind My Testimonies

Testimony # 1

"I stand in faith believing."

In 2002, I received news from my doctors that changed the trajectory of my life. They said, "You have a sick heart that will not get better. Eventually, you may need a heart transplant." What do you do with this kind of news? I was 27 years old. I just started a new career in teaching. I was working on my master's degree. I became the father of a beautiful baby girl. "Wow, Wow," I cried. I asked myself, "What do I do? How do I make it through this unexpected storm in my life?" I could give in to fear or become a courageous warrior and fight for my life. I chose to fight and pray by putting on the whole armor of God and taking every spiritual weapon in my possession to fight and stand against the fiery darts of the devil. I fought with the shield of faith, the Word of God, and prayed in the Spirit with all kinds of prayers and requests. This process did not happen overnight. It took time for me to get to this level of fighting and faith.

As years passed, my heart became weaker. I found myself surrendering my will to God's will and ending up in my "nevertheless moment." I began learning how to pray and grow my faith and trust in God.

In 2011, I said to my mother in one of the darkest moments of my life, "I do not know why God chose me for this tedious journey. I did not ask for it, nor am I equipped for such a journey. But I know, if God is on this journey with me and He is plotting the course, steering the boat, and knows my destination, I will be all right. I understand what the doctors are telling us, but I know that God has the last word about my life. I am not afraid of dying. I have had many conversations with God about my life. He knows my heart's desires and what I believe Him to accomplish. Yes, I want to be around to raise my girls, watch them grow into womanhood, and fulfill their dreams. I want to have a long life and live out my Bible age years and beyond in good health, but I am all right. I am in God's hands. I cannot lose either way, whether I am on this side or the other side of Glory. There is assurance and healing in God's hands. So, what better place to be than to be held by Him and believing and standing on His promises."

> "Trials are intended to make us think, to wean us from the world, to send us to the Bible, to drive us to our knees."
>
> -
>
> **J.C. Ryle**

Testimony #2

"I believe in the wonder-working power of God."

After being diagnosed, my heart became weaker and larger over the years. In 2009, the doctors implanted a combined pacemaker and defibrillator in my chest due to heart failure. After the implant, blood clots formed in my lungs followed by an infection and debilitating pain that racked my body.

My mother said, "Son, if I could take away the pain and bear it myself, I would." I said to my mother, "I would not wish this pain on anyone. I am going to be all right. Just hold me in prayer."

The powerful morphine drips were not bringing much relief, and the different medications for the infection were not efficiently working. My temperature continued to spike. The nurses kept packing my body with ice and trying to bring my fever down.

After being placed on blood clot medication, the doctors told me one afternoon, "Things are not working as fast as we hoped. We do not want to operate, but we may have to because we do not want a clot to move to your heart or brain. You have a lot going on in your body. The problems we are facing are your weak body, the infection, and of course, your weak heart. We are giving you the most powerful antibiotics to treat the infection. There is one treatment left that we have not tried. However, if we give you this treatment, there would be no recourse left to treat the infection if you get worse."

The doctors continued, "We will watch you throughout the night and decide on a course of action tomorrow morning. This is serious, but hopefully the antibiotics will work by morning."

Later that night, I started getting worse. I was going in and out of consciousness.

My mother told me weeks later what transpired that night. She said, "I just sat by your bedside praying while you kept holding and squeezing my hand in time of excruciating pain. After you finally went to sleep, I tried to get some rest. The nurses, Yoni and Andy (two of my best friends who stayed for days with me) kept changing your clothes every 30 minutes due to the fever and your sweating.

Hours later, I heard Yoni say to Andy, 'He is getting hotter. We have changed his clothing and bedding twice in less than an hour. We better call the nurse.' I got up to go over to your bed, but the Holy Spirit said, 'Sit back down. I will tell you when to move. Let your friends and the nurses attend to him.'"

My mother continued, "In obedience, I did not move from the chair, but went into the spiritual realm through prayer, asking God to deliver you from the attacks of blood clots, the infection, and the pain. I plead the blood of Jesus over your body and stood on Psalms 91. Around 5am, the Holy Spirit instructed me to get up and stand by your bedside and call you out from your comatose state. At this point, all you could do was make very faint sounds. You were too weak to open your eyes or move any part of your body."

"The Holy Spirit instructed me to call out your name three times, and then lay my right hand on your chest and pray. In obedience, I said, 'Markel come out, Markel come out, Markel come out in Jesus' Name. This is your mother speaking, open your eyes, you can do it.' Immediately, your eyes started opening a little, but they rolled back and were very yellow. I said to you, 'Keep your eyes open for your mother.' I laid my right hand on your chest over the incision and started praying again. As I was praying, my hand started getting fiery hot as if it were in a furnace. I did not know what was happening, but I kept on praying in obedience. By the time I finished praying, your eyes had opened. However, your voice was still weak."

"By the time the doctors came into the room at 6am, your temperature had stabilized and you were talking with your eyes open.

The doctors said to you, 'You had us worried there for a while. We are glad to see your temperature is normal and have stabilized.' After they checked you out, they said, 'We will keep an eye on you for the next few days, hoping things will continue to go in the right direction.' In a week, you were able to go home with a blood thinner and you were on the road to recovery."

My mother told me, "I know that prayer works. I know that the power of God transcends and defies our human logic. I cannot explain why my hand exploded in heat while I was praying for you. At first, I asked myself, 'Was it the heat from your body or was it the heat from the Holy Spirit working through my hand?' Since 2009, this has happened to me on two other occasions."

I know that God operates in our faith and obedience and the Holy Spirit can operate through us to aid others

---

TRIALS

"The trials you encounter will introduce you to your strength."

-

Epictetus

Testimony #3

"In the darkest moments of my life, when my spirit was wounded; my soul was shaken; my strength was ebbing, and my faith was wavering, I fell on my knees and poured out my soul before God. I did the messy pouring. I poured out worry, grief, hurt, doubt, anger, and trouble all over the place. As I was pouring from the depth of pain, God was wiping up my mess and filling me with his love, mercy, grace, and assurance for my journey." –
Markel Crockton

In 2013, after several years of medication management and many hospitalizations, the Ejection Fraction (EF) function of my heart became less than twelve percent. I was taking over eighty pills a day for survival. Just one of my medications cost over $6,000.00 each month. For many days, I was living on sheer will, but I refused to give up on life.

Finally, I had to get an artificial heart, called a LVAD (left ventricular assist device), which is a mechanical device placed inside my chest until a heart became available.

Unfortunately, the first LVAD failed. Three weeks later, with my body still frail, I had to go through a second eight-hour operation to replace the LVAD pump. The device was causing clotting in the device. The doctors were afraid a clot could travel to my brain. Therefore, the only course of action was to operate again.

The LVAD is a scientific gift to prolong life until a heart becomes available for some patients. Some patients live with the device for life because a heart transplant is not an option for them.

The pump had its challenges, especially for my family. I needed someone to be with me most of the time because I was hooked up to batteries during the day and to electrical outlets during the night to power the cells. The batteries had a charged life of approximately eight hours. I was always connected to four batteries and carried four to eight batteries with me. Before I left the hospital, my social worker informed the local electricity company that I always needed electrical service and they had to call me for suspected storms or power outages. We were told to purchase a generator for backup in case of a power outage. The local fire department was informed of my condition. I was told that at least one person at the station had training on the device. With power cords coming out from my side, they had to be cleaned nightly in a sterile environment to keep me from getting an infection. My family had to learn how to take care of my wounds and know what to do if the device failed.

Simple tasks like taking a shower became a big ordeal. It took up to 45 minutes just to get the device, cords, and incisions covered and wrapped. Getting into the shower and bathing could take up to another 30 minutes. This was why the medical staff suggested taking a shower twice a week. Simple things I could do in the past and on my own now became arduous.

While waiting for a heart, I got a blood clot in my brain as a result of the LVAD and had to have emergency brain surgery that lasted over 10 hours. I found out later that they thought they had lost me on the operating table because there was so much bleeding in my brain.

From this operation, I walked around with half of my skull missing for months. I wore and slept in a helmet to protect my head. I had to learn how to walk and make sense of simple things after the operation.

I tried not to complain. I thanked God for my life, the process, my family, and the medical staff who were taking good care of my medical needs. God was in control of all my needs. The Word of God in Psalms 34:8 says, *"Taste and see that the Lord is good."*

Praise and worship are the weapons of warfare.

Testimony #4

"I refuse to doubt God."
"I will praise Him for my victory before my manifestation."

On February 19, 2014, I went to the emergency room due to a headache that was getting worse. We were told to watch out for any change of color in my urine. Any dark brown urine could mean clotting in the LVAD. There was no change in the color of my urine.

We were told that LVAD patients had a 12% chance of a brain bleed so the odds were low. I was one of the twelve percenters. If I had known that the first sign of a headache could have meant clotting in my brain, I would have rushed to the hospital immediately, not waiting for days thinking I had a slight cold or a sinus infection. After calling the doctors about the headaches, they thought I had a cold and told me to watch out for fever or change in my urine color.

Even after I arrived in the emergency room, the doctors were not thinking of a brain bleed. They were checking my heart and the numbers on my LVAD thinking that it was my heart device. My friend, who came with me to the emergency room and who once worked in the neurology department at another hospital, kept insisting that they do a CT on my head.

I was complaining about the pain getting worse so one doctor decided to take a CT scan of my head. Within minutes, doctors were coming from all over the place in my room. "What is going on?" I asked. The doctors told me that they had less than two hours to reverse the blood thinner, Warfarin, in my body and get me to surgery. It was very serious. The scan revealed a big blood clot in my brain.

I said to my mother, "Gee, why am I continuously being attacked? What is going on? It seems like Satan wants to take me out."

In the meantime, my male ER nurse had to pump an injection manually to reverse the warfarin and prepare me for surgery. The drip coming from my IV was not fast enough to reverse the warfarin promptly. He was pumping so hard that he was drenched in sweat. He kept saying, "I got to get this done. We only have minutes to get you to the operating room. Time is of the essence." My mother was praying and laying hands on me not caring about the team of doctors and nurses around me. She said, "I got work to do also."

The neurosurgeon came down and told me what was happening in my head and what to expect. He said, "With an artificial heart device, a massive blood clot in your brain, and a very short window to operate, the odds are against you. We have a team ready for you, and I will do my best to get you back to your family." He told my mother and daughters to kiss me and say their goodbyes. Of course, my mother prayed down heaven in a few words. I knew they were in a daze as they wheeled me away. No one had time to process what was happening. My daughters were asking their Grandma, "Is Daddy going to be, okay?"

What do you do when storms keep on raging in your life?

You will read more about my journey from my mother's journal later in this book.

PRAYER
Father God, You know me so well. You created me. You know my name and all about me. You know my thoughts and what I am believing You to accomplish in my health. You know my situation and with what I am wrestling. You know where all of my hurts, pains, and sadness, reside within me. So, I am here in Your presence with great confidence knowing You GOT ME!

-

Markel Crockton

Testimony #5

The Call
"I walk in praise and thanksgiving."

On October 1, 2014, at 9:00 am, a heart became available. My doctor called and told me to get to the hospital within the hour. He asked, "Do you accept the heart?" I was in shock and could not speak. "Are you there? You do not seem excited?" "Yes, I am here and excited, but is there someone else sicker than I am who needs it more than I do?" The doctor said, "You need the heart now. If you decline, it means you will go back to the bottom of the list and may not get this opportunity again. Do you understand what this means?" My mother, who was on the call said, "We will be there at the hospital within the hour." The call was bittersweet. Someone had to die for me to get their heart.

My mother said, "Life and death is God's business and in His hands. Accept the gift, thank God for it, honor the family and donor by taking good care of the present, and live a life worthy of it."

After a seven hours operation, I woke up with a new, unknown heart beating in my body.

I walk daily in gratitude with a heart of thanksgiving and a mouth of praise. I am thankful for God's healing power, the prayers of the saints, and the family who made their 29-year-old son's heart available so that I could get a second chance at life.

I do not take life for granted. I know I have been given a precious gift. After five major surgeries, I am in the land of the living doing well because of God's grace and mercy.

Andrae Crouch's song, *"Through It All,"* puts so many of my testimonies in perspective. To my readers, please find and sing *"Through It All"* to experience this powerful song for yourself.

PART II

FROM MY MOTHER'S JOURNAL ABOUT MY JOURNEY

Introduction

"If the Holy Spirit should come and begin to preach to your heart, giving you rich and enlightened thoughts, ... be quiet and listen to him who can talk better than you, and note what he proclaims and write it down,"
- Martin Luther

Months before my son's diagnosis of heart failure, God warned me that something was about to happen. I did not know what it was, but the Holy Spirit revealed and instructed me what I should know and do.

The Holy Spirit revealed:

Revelation #1

You will be in seasons of spiritual warfare, and I need you to shut things down and listen to ME. The devil desires to sift you and your son like wheat, but I got you both in the palm of my hand.

Instruction...

Be strong in the Lord** and the power of His might. Put on the **whole armor of God** that you may be **able to stand** against the wiles of the devil. For we do not wrestle against flesh and blood, but against principalities, against powers, against the rulers of the darkness of this age, against spiritual hosts - **Ephesians 6:10-20

Revelation #2

Listen to my voice. I will speak to you plainly from my Word, from your prayers, and through visions. In time, you will see My Glory revealed unto you.

"He that hath ears to hear let him hear," - ***Matthew 11:15***

Revelation #3

Do not be moved by what your natural eyes will see. Satan wants to plant fear and blind you from seeing Me. Natural sight can be deceiving. You are to stand on My word.

"*Walk by faith and not by sight,*" II Corinthians 5:7

Revelation #4

Keep Track of my Revelations to you.

Keep a journal with you always - in your car, near your bed, in your purse. Write when I instruct you to write. Listen when I tell you to listen. Know my voice and adhere to it.

Over the years, God had revealed himself to me about many things, but not at this level of specificity.

Through God's revelation and instructions for my journey with my son, God was with us in every detail working out things for my son and instructing me what to do.

- **Liz Crockton**

Fear not, for I am with you. Be not dismayed, for I am your God. I will strengthen you. Yes, I will help you, I will uphold you with my righteous right hand.
-
Isaiah 41:10

My Son's Journey: 2010 Journal Entries

HEALING HANDS 2010

Hospital

The second time my right hand became as hot as fire was in 2010. My son is back in the hospital for a procedure due to heart failure. The doctors said his heart is getting weaker.

I walked into his room around 6:45 am, and he was awake. The Holy Spirit said, "Do not have your usual morning talks at this time. Put your things down on the chair and have Morning Prayer first. Lay your right hand on his chest where he has had the procedure and pray." Again, being obedient to the voice of God, I said to him, "God is speaking to me to lay my hand on the place you had the surgery and pray." He said, "Go ahead, Mom," his usual line for most things I asked of him. I laid my hand on his chest and started praying. For the second time, my hand became as hot as fire as I was praying. Also, I could feel his body in that area getting hotter and hotter as if it wanted to catch on fire in that area.

I finished praying. I was looking around the room, not sure what I was looking for, and wondered if my son felt what just happened. We both were quiet for a long time. I went back to my chair and just started praising God and reading my Bible. Later, during the day, I said to him, "The strangest thing happened this morning while I was praying for you. My hand became hot as fire, and so was the area of your body I was praying over." My son said, "I felt it too as you were praying. Your side got hotter and hotter, and I could feel the fire as if it were the power of God all over my body. What was that? Has this happened to you before?" I said, "Yes, when you were in the hospital last year with that severe infection and the blood clot in your lungs. You were too sick to know what was happening."

My Son's Journey: 2011 Journal Entries

Prayer Time

Tuesday, September 6, 2011

9:58am
Hospital Waiting Room

Good Morning Heavenly Father,

We bless your holy name.

*Your Word in **1 Timothy 6:17** says, "You giveth us richly all things to enjoy."*

In You, we enjoy a reasonable portion of health, strength, gifts, and talents.

In You, we enjoy the gift of life. In You, we enjoy air to breathe, water to drink, and food to eat. We appreciate the beauty of your art of majestic mountains, blue skies, and running streams. In You, we enjoy the seasons of summer, spring, winter and fall and all the beauty that each season brings—pure white snow, changing colors in leaves, flowers blooming in spring, and hummingbirds that sing.

I testify of your goodness. You make our crooked road straight. You provide water in our drylands. You are our Bridge over troubled waters. You are our constant help in times of need. You are our shelter in times of storms. You carry our heavy load and bear our burdens. We thank you.

I thank you for my son, Markel. You know his secret thoughts and fears. Strengthen his faith in You. I stand on Your Word declaring that no good thing is withheld from him. In faith, I know, that I know, his heart is healed, or you have a new heart here on earth for him. I am giving You the "now" praise for the "yet" praise to come for his new heart.

Thank you for blessing him in mighty ways. In sickness, You healed him. In disappointment, You picked him up and refreshed his spirit. In pain, You granted him relief. In loneliness, You give him peace. In financial situations, You opened the floodgates of Heaven and poured him out blessings, after blessings, after blessings. You granted help with excellent health insurance. You have provided him with some of the best doctors in the world. You presented him with his own home, a car to drive, an excellent credit report, beautiful children, and an excellent education from some of the best schools and universities. You spared his life from the sometimes mean and violent streets of this city. But most of all, You saved his soul. You forgave him of his sins and granted him new mercies. I thank you.

Now Father God, protect, bless, and be with Markel as he goes through this procedure today. Encamp your angels of protection around him to guide the doctors, nurses, and medical staff as they minister unto him. We thank you for a clean report, and count it done, because Your Word in Romans 4:17, says, **"Calleth those things which be not as though they were." In Jesus' name, we pray. Amen!**

Don't neglect or minimize
the power of prayer.
Your prayers in the ears of God
have the power to change and
rearrange your situation in an
instant. PRAY!

-
Minister Liz Crockton

Monday, October 3, 2011

8:49am
Hospital Waiting Room

Psalm 91: 1 KJV: *He that dwelleth in the secret place of the Most High shall abide under the shadow of the Almighty.*

Good morning Heavenly Father,

I bless Your name. Thank You for allowing me to enter Your presence and Your court with praise and thanksgiving this morning. Thank You for Your Word.

Your Word tells me that You are my son's refuge, his place of safety, and You are his God. Your Word also tells me though ten thousand are dying around him, the evil will not touch him- for You are his Jehovah. You said, "You have ordered Your angels to protect him wherever he goes." Thank you. You said, "Your angels will steady him with their hands to keep him from stumbling against the rocks of life."

You said that he can "safely meet a lion or step on poisonous snakes, and can trample them beneath his feet, and You will rescue him."

God, you said, "When he calls on You, You will answer him, be with him in times of trouble, rescue him, honor him, and satisfy him with a full and long life and show him your salvation." I claim it done, I receive it, believe it, and know that it will be with my son. Amen.

Monday, October 3, 2011
9:39am
Bedroom at Home

Markel's Medicine

God is speaking to my spirit again this morning. He is telling me to go into my son's room, lift his medicines toward heaven, and pray.

Presently, my son takes eighty-nine pills daily due to his cardiomyopathy. I jokingly said, only the doctors and nurses can pronounce the names of some of these medicines. At times, some nurses struggle to pronounce the correct name.

We walk by faith in taking any medication. What are the properties or compounds in each pill? What harm are they doing to our body?

Father God,

Good morning again! You spoke to my spirit a few moments ago, and told me to go to my son's room, gather up all his medicines, lift them before You, and pray that they would do what they were designed, and do him no harm.

I thank You for his medicines. I thank You for the knowledge given to those who have the gift of science, research, and know how to create drugs that provide relief and healing.

Right now, Father God, I am standing on Your Word because I know it cannot return void.

*Your Word says in **Exodus 15:26**: that I am the Lord who heals You. Thank You for Your healing power in Markel's life.*

*You said in **Psalms 118:17**: that my son should not die but live to tell of all the work and deeds of the Lord. I thank You.*

Isaiah 53 5: *You said, "He was wounded for our transgressions, He was bruised for our iniquities: the chastisement of our peace was upon him, and with his stripes, we are healed." I know that my son is healed. Thank you.*

Your Word also tells us in **Isaiah 58:8:** *"Then shall thy light break forth as the morning, and thine health shall spring forth speedily: and thy righteousness shall go before thee; the glory of the Lord shall be thy reward."*

In expectancy, we believe Your light shall break forth like the morning in Markel's life. His healing shall spring forth speedily, and righteousness shall go before him, and the glory of the Lord will be his reward.

We claim Your Word to be so in Jesus' Name, Amen!

God's Healing Medicine

God revealed to me that Markel is to take spiritual Medicine (His Word) daily for his soul, just as he must take natural medicine for his condition. Just as his doctors are prescribing medications (some by trial and error, with adjustments, hoping they will work for him) "I," Doctor Jesus, "am going to prescribe daily medicine for him to take by faith. My medicine has the power to perform what it promised. It works quickly, is powerful, and needs no changes or adjustments. The more he takes, the stronger he will get in me."

Administer these Word pills with faith and prayer, so that the Word of God and the promises of God will produce unshakeable faith and confidence in him to fight, stand, and travail.

Psalm 37:4

"Delight thyself also in the Lord: and he shall give thee the desires of thine heart."

Isaiah 41:13

"For I, the Lord thy God will hold thy right hand, saying unto thee, Fear not; I will help thee."

Psalm 18:2

"The Lord is my rock, and my fortress, and my deliverer; my God, my strength, in whom I will trust."

Psalm 91:15-16

"He shall call upon me, and I will answer him: I will be with him in trouble; I will deliver him and honor him. With long life will I satisfy him and shew him my salvation."

Isaiah 55:9-11 - *For as the heavens are higher than the earth, so are my ways higher than your ways, and my thoughts than your thoughts. For as the rain cometh down, and the snow from heaven, and returneth not thither, but watereth the earth, and maketh it bring forth and bud, that it may give seed to the sower, and bread to the eater: So shall my word be that goeth forth out of my mouth: it shall not return unto me void, but it shall accomplish that which I please, and it shall prosper in the thing whereto I sent it.*

3 John 2 - *"Beloved, I wish above all things that thou mayest prosper and be in health, even as thy soul prospereth."*

Romans 8:38-39 - *For I am persuaded, that neither death, nor life, nor angels, nor principalities, nor powers, nor things present, nor things to come, nor height, nor depth, nor any other creature, shall be able to separate us from the love of God, which is in Christ Jesus our Lord.*

Jeremiah: 29:11: *For I know the thoughts that I think toward you, saith the Lord, thoughts of peace, and not of evil, to give you an expected end.*

Philippians 4:6 - *Be careful about nothing, but in everything by prayer and supplication with thanksgiving let your requests be made known unto God.*

Psalms 38:9 - *Lord, all my desire is before thee; and my groaning is not hidden from thee.*

Ephesians 3:20 - *Now unto him, that is able to do exceedingly abundantly above all that we ask or think, according to the power that worketh in us.*

Proverbs 18:21 - *Death and life are in the power of the tongue: and they that love it shall eat the fruit thereof.*

My Son's Journey: 2012 Journal Entries

9:30am
Waiting Room Hospital

This morning at 5:00 a.m., Markel was taken to surgery to have an LVAD, an artificial heart placed in his chest. His heart has become so weak that only the medicine is doing the pumping for his heart. This device can help keep him alive until he can get a heart.

They are getting ready to take him to surgery. We just prayed and then he had a little talk with his daughters.

My church family at Twelfth Baptist Church in Boston, my prayer warriors in various states, and my family were praying with us on his behalf. I placed him in the hands of God, wiped the little tear from my eye, and prayed my prayer... *"Lord, please save my son and send your angels of protection to stand guard over him."*

At 9:30 a.m., while Markel was still in surgery, my spirit became restless as if I knew something was going wrong in the operating room. I did not know what it was. I tried to shake it off, and it would not leave.

I tried praying and singing but could not focus. I made a request of the Lord to let me visualize what was going on in the operation room. God allowed me to see shadows of what was happening.

Around 9:35 a.m., my niece, Tracy, called from North Carolina, praying in the spirit. I said, "Hello, hello," but she was crying and praying in spiritual tongues. I do not know what she was saying because I do not have the gift of speaking in a tongue or interpreting what is being said. At that moment, I knew that God was warning us to pray and intercede on Markel's behalf. I just started praying with her for the next 30 minutes. After we finished, she said "My spirit is troubled. The devil wants to bring harm to Markel and is trying to take him out. We are in warfare. I got to go and call my prayer warriors to get on the case. I will call you later."

> "Prayer Warriors go before God, their Commander and Chief, and report for duty on the battle ground of prayer and faith, knowing God has provided them with protected armor and the right weapons for battle…the Helmet of salvation; the Breastplate of Righteousness; the Girdle of Truth; the Sandals of Peace; the Shield of Faith; and the Sword of the Spirit.
> Prayer Warriors don't give up or retreat because the battle gets rough. They know they will get battle wounds, battle scars, battle defeats or battle fatigue. They know that God will bind their wounds, heal their bodies, and restore their strength to fight until the victory is won."
>
> - ***Minister Liz Crockton***

Prayer Time
Almighty God,

Allow me in your presence right now. I need you. Markel requires you. The surgeons need you. Something is going wrong in the operating room. Disperse Markel's angel of protection to stand guard over him right now and deliver him from any evil. You have already spoken to me through your Word and said that You will keep him from all harm and You will watch over his life. You told me to stand on Your promise and to walk by faith and not by sight. You have warned me not to be moved by what I see when my son comes out of the operating room. I believe Your word will not return void but will accomplish its purpose. Therefore, on the authority of Your word, Jesus took our infirmities and bore our sickness. In faith, believing Markel is redeemed from the curse of disease.

I thank you for now, and what you are doing in that operating room at this moment. Amen!

- My other niece from Boston called and said that she had been in prayer with her friend around 10:00 a.m. because her spirit was troubled. "What is going on? Whatever is happening the devil is a liar. He cannot have my cousin." I told her to keep on praying and believing God to do the miraculous.

- A few minutes ago, after over ten hours in surgery, the surgeon came to the waiting room and told me they had finished, and he was in the ICU. However, he said, "His heart was so huge that they had problems getting him to tolerate the breathing machine. As a result, we had to do a whole new procedure and ditch the one he and the team had practiced. He will be fine and you will be able to see him in a few hours. Do you have any questions for me?" He asked. All I could say was, "Thank you, thank you, thank you." I am too exhausted to think.

Check-up Today

News

I was told today by one of his doctors, after four months, that they lost my son on the operation table and had to revive him twice...*but God said...*

> ***Jesus replied, "What is impossible with man is possible with God,"***
>
> -
>
> **Luke 18:27**

My Son's Journey: 2013 Journal Entries

September 30, 2013
7:00 p.m.
Hospital

Watch and Pray
1 Peter 5:8: *"Be sober, be vigilant; because of your adversary the devil, as a roaring lion..."*

Markel is recuperating from his first heart surgery and is doing great. He is doing better than expected, so I am going home, taking a shower, getting some rest, and coming back early in the morning. He said, "Mom, I need you to be with me in prayer all night tonight. Do not be alarmed. I am okay, but something seems wrong in this room. I need you with me." Usually, he wants me to go home and rest when he is doing well. "I know you're exhausted and was looking forward to your bed tonight after being here for weeks, but I need you."

I did not ask what was going on in his spirit, but I knew it was something. I knew that through prayer and obedience, God would intervene and bind the enemy's plot against my son.

I took my phone out of my purse and set the alarm to ring every hour until dawn.

    7:45pm

    8:45pm

    9:45pm

    10:45pm

    11:45pm

    12:45am

1:45am

2:45am

3:45am

4:45am

5:45am

6:45am

7:45am

At 7:25pm, I started making a list of the things I thought I should be praying for each hour. I started writing and wrote:

- Pray for what is causing him fear
- Pray for his heart function and oxygen level to remain normal

Before I could write the next thing down, the Lord spoke to my spirit and said, "Put an **"X"** through your list and pray about the items on the list I am about to give you. Write down the following and pray about them throughout the night:

1. **MY PRESENCE IN THE ROOM (God's Presence)**
2. **MERCY**
3. **GRACE**
4. **HEALING**
5. **PROTECTION**
6. **YOUR SON'S FAITH**
7. **YOUR FAITH**

Each time you pray, get up, and go over to his bed and lay your hands on him.

I did what I was instructed to do. I was given seven specific things to pray for during those 12 hours.

During the night, I prayed, read Scriptures, hummed hymns, and talked to God through my journal.

Markel drifted off to sleep around 11:00pm and slept like a baby throughout the night.

Samuel Chadwick wrote, *"The most important part of prayer is not what we say to God, but what God says to us."*

At 7:45pm: I prayed for God's presence and strong faith

Father God,

Your Word says in Isaiah 41:10: "Fear thou not; for I am with thee: be not dismayed; for I am thy God: I will strengthen thee; yea, I will help thee; yea, I will uphold thee with the right hand of my righteousness." Father, I ask for Your presence in this room. I know You are with us and have never left us. Strengthen Markel's faith to fight and resist the devil. Whatever spirit is not of You in this place, by the authority of the blood of Jesus, I bind it in Jesus' name. BE GONE!! Father God, loose your peace and protection in this place and over my son. Amen!

At 8:45pm, I focused on God's grace and mercy through Scripture and songs.

I read, *"It is of the Lord's mercies that we are not consumed because his compassions fail not. They are new every morning: great is thy faithfulness."* (Lamentations 3:22-23 KJV). I softly sang the song, *Your Grace and Mercy*, written by Franklin Williams. To my readers, please find the lyrics of this beautiful song to help you focus on God's grace and mercy in your life.

At 9:45pm, I prayed the Word of God in Isaiah 54:17

Father God, I stand on Your word that, "No weapon that formed against thee (Markel) shall prosper, and every tongue that shall rise against thee (him) in judgment thou shalt condemn. This is the heritage of the servants of the Lord, and their righteousness is of me, saith the Lord. Amen! Isaiah 54:17 KJV

At 10:45pm, I prayed the prayer of protection - Psalms 91:1-5

"He that dwelleth in the secret place of the Most High shall abide under the shadow of the Almighty. I will say of the Lord; He is my refuge and my fortress: my God; in him will I trust. Surely, he shall deliver thee from the snare of the fowler, and from the noisome pestilence. He shall cover thee with his feathers, and under his wings shalt thou trust: his truth shall be thy shield and buckler. Thou shalt not be afraid for the terror by night; nor for the arrow that flieth by day." (Psalms 91:1-5).

At 11:45pm, I stood on God's Word of faith and prayed - Matthew 9:21-22

And Jesus answered them, "Truly, I say to you, if you have faith and do not doubt, you will not only do what has been done to the fig tree but even if you say to this mountain, 'Be taken up and thrown into the sea,' it will happen. And whatever you ask in prayer, you will receive, if you have faith."

Jesus turned and seeing her he said, "Take heart, daughter; your faith has made you well." And instantly the woman was made well.

Father God, concerning my faith, if you said it, I know you will do it. You said, "Whatever you ask in prayer, you will receive if you have faith." Father God, I have faith in You. I know You will not hold any good thing from me, and You will perform Your word in my life.

At 12:45am, I prayed for the presence of God through His Word

Father God, thank you for Your presence in this room. I affirm that You are our ever-present help. Do not cast me away from Your presence, and do not take Your Holy Spirit from me (Psalms 51:11). Behold, I stand at the door and knock: if any man hears my voice, and open the door, I will come into him and will sup with him, and he with me (Revelation 3:20). Therefore, brethren, having the boldness to enter the Holiest by the blood of Jesus, let us draw near with a true heart in full assurance of faith, having our hearts sprinkled from an evil conscience and our bodies washed with pure water (Hebrews 10:19-22).

At 1:45am, I prayed for healing

God warns His Children

John 16:13 - *Howbeit when he, the Spirit of truth, is come, he will guide you into all truth: for he shall not speak of himself; but whatsoever he shall hear, that shall he speak and he will shew you things to come. The Holy Spirit will speak to our spirit and tell us things to come.*

From 2:45am to 7:45am, I prayed and continued to read God's word over my son.

August 19, 2013

Sitting on my back deck gazing at the trees

I wrote this prayer out of the depth of my heart thanking God for allowing me to stand by my son for his healing and trusting Him for a heart transplant.

My Prayer:

"God writes the Gospel not in the Bible alone, but also on trees, and in the flowers and clouds and stars." — Martin Luther

Father God,

Just like a tree that is planted by the water, I shall not be moved. I thank you for your standing grace. I thank you for the unmovable favor. I thank you for the many ways you continue to speak to me through your created art... the trees. As I sit quietly on my back porch gazing at the beauty and strength of your trees, I am thankful that you have allowed me to stand like the trees of old…strong, unmovable, and tall. Through many storms of life, through all kinds of weather, tossed around, bents, and parts are broken, yet you keep me standing like the trees of time. I am thankful that you have planted me deep in stable soil … deep in your word… deep in the gift of prayer and wrapped in your mercy and grace. Father God, in trials and storms, you have helped me to stand my ground, rooted in faith and not sway to the pressures of life. I am thankful for your holding power. I am grateful for the lessons you continue to reveal through your creation.

In Jesus' Name I pray, Amen.

"Whenever you get into the presence of God, the impossible becomes possible, the unknowns are revealed, and His love wraps you in the cradle of His arms."

-

Minister Liz Crockton

My Son's Journey: 2014 Journal Entries

Friday morning, February 21, 2014
Intensive Care Unit – After surgery

The nurses allowed me in the ICU to see my son for a few minutes. They were working on him. I am thankful that God had warned me not to be deceived by the things I would witness by my eyes.

I went back to the waiting room and wrote in my journal.

Father God,

I bless Your name this day. You are God and worthy of all our praise. I thank You for Your Word earlier this morning that You will keep my son from all harm and that You would watch over his life in the operating room. You told me not to be moved by what I would see with my natural eyes. Satan wants me to think the worst and lose faith by what my eyes would behold. You said physical sight could be deceiving. I was to stand on Your Word in II Corinthians 5:7: "We walk by faith and not by sight."

Although, I barely recognize my son from all the tubes, wires, bags of so many medicines, bleeding, and the swelling in his head...my God. I acknowledge Your handiwork and hands all over his body. He looks good. He is alive. Thank You. In Jesus' name. Amen!

Saturday, February 22, 2014

7:45am
Intensive Care Unit

Outside of Markel's window in the ICU, I see three little birds sitting on the ledge playing and singing. What are they doing out there in the dead of winter? Why three? Why are they so happy? I went behind the head of his bed and tapped on the window, but they did not fly away.

I mention this because my sister, Dot, used to call and tell me about one little bird that would come and sing outside of her bedroom window every morning while she was battling cancer. She would wonder what God was trying to tell her. I went down to see her before her surgery, and sure enough, this same little bird came each morning playing and singing.

I have no explanation and no revelation about this.

8:00am

I sat back down in my chair next to my son's bed. I picked up my Bible to read. I heard God's voice say, "Clear out your Bible from clutter. Hold me close. Now eat the word from Jeremiah 5:14b; *"I will make my words in your mouth like fire."*

Sunday, February 23, 2014

Hospital
10:00am

Psalms 46:1, 8, 10-11

God is our refuge and strength, Come and see the works of the Lord. Be still and know that I am God. The Lord Almighty is with us.

Psalms 91:15-16

He will call upon me, and I will answer him; I will be with him in trouble.

I will deliver him and honor him; with long life will I satisfy him and show him my salvation.

> ***"I refuse to doubt God."***
>
> ***"I will praise Him for my victory even before my manifestation."***
>
> \-
>
> **Markel Crockton**

Sunday, February 23, 2014

Hospital
10:00pm

Father God, I know that You know all things. Please stop these seizures my son keeps having and heal him from this. The doctors say this is not good for him to keep having these seizures. As I was praying, a word came from the Lord.

A word from the Lord:

"I know the plan I have for your son's life. He will be blessed with a long life. Write down what I am speaking to you. Liz, Do you trust Me? Do you believe Me? Do you trust Me?"

"Yes, Lord, I trust you with my life…I trust you."

"Let Me finish doing My work through him. Don't you want to see Michael and his whole family come to Christ?"

"Yes, Lord. Martez and his family?" "Yes, Lord." "Trust me. Don't you know I am the same God who parted the Red Sea and Jordan River? Don't you know I will part the troubling water in your son's life to get him through to his healing? Why do you think I considered my son Markel for this journey? For my glory and honor and to draw others unto me. He will testify of my goodness. Don't you know that pain and suffering is never wasted for those I love?"

I started crying before the Lord in prayer. I prayed:

Father God, please forgive me for giving in to fear. I trust you. In Jesus' Name.

As I was praying, I saw a vision of a long white robe. The hem of the garment stretched out to me to grab and hold. I could feel the sensation of the pain in my hand from grabbing on and holding on so tight.

The seizures subsided, and some of the swellings started going down.

Sunday, February 23, 2014

11:00pm
Intensive Care Unit

Markel is alert.

"Mom, are you okay? Do you need anything?" I said, "No, do not worry about me, I am okay. Rest and get better for me." In a faint voice: "Okay." Are you going to stay with me all night?" "I will not leave your side." "Good." "Are you sure you will be here in the morning?' "Right here in the chair staring at your handsome face."

Prayer Time

James 5:16

Father God, I thank you and give you praises for the privilege of seeing my son alive to witness a brand-new day and new mercies.

I thank you for providing for all his needs during his health storm.

Thank you for keeping his emotions calm from the pain raging in his body.

Thank you for keeping his mind and thoughts in perfect peace and from fear, as he heals.

I thank You for medicine that releases pain and help to bring forth healing and comfort. I thank You for the medical procedures, CT scans, MRI, and X-rays made available to him. We thank You for the skillful hands and medical knowledge You have loaned unto doctors and nurses and all those who serve in the medical field helping him in his time of need.

But I am so thankful to You, Doctor Jesus, our doctor above all doctors. You can go where medicine cannot reach. You can see what machines cannot. There is nothing hidden from You about my son. You made him and knew all about him. While doctors are still trying to figure things out, You have already worked out his healing and health plan. I thank You. Amen!

Off the Transplant List

After Markel was released from the ICU neurology unit, he was sent back to the Cardiac Care Unit. One of the lead doctors on his LVAD team told me, "You know we had to take Markel off the heart transplant list."

"What are you saying to me," I asked.

She answered, "Because of the brain bleed and all that he is going through, we cannot be sure of his outcome so we took him off the list. We are so sorry." (At this time, we were not told that Markel had suffered several mini strokes. We learned this information months later.)

I thought, "He fought so hard and did the things necessary to get on the list, now this?"

While she was speaking these words to me, I refused to receive her words in my spirit. I knew what God had promised me, and what I believed God to do. If God said it, I knew that he would do it. I knew God would not withhold any good things from my son and He would perform His word in his life. When you are in a storm, you must trust God in all things. You cannot be a doubter. You must have spiritual ears to hear.

I went to the Hospital Chapel and prayed:

Father God,

I have faith and peace in You. I stand on Your Word in Mark 11:24: Therefore, I say unto you, what things ye desire when ye pray, believe that ye receive them, and ye shall have them.

Father God, send my son's angels to come against any hindrance or weapon set against him in receiving a new heart. I declare in the name of Jesus that every plot or scheme of Satan against my son canceled in the name of Jesus.

Father, please continue to give me a spiritual ear to hear what You are saying to me. Grant me spiritual eyes to see those things that are not yet revealed. Touch my feet to stand steadfast in You and Your Word. I pray in Jesus Name!

Answered Prayer

Let me testify about God's Power. Before the end of the day, less than 6 hours, they came back to me and said, "We have placed him back on the heart transplant list. We are not sure why he was taken off. We are so proud of this news for Markel. He is such a fighter."

I said, "God is good. Thank you all so much for what you are doing and the excellent level of care the team is providing for my son." As a mother, I bear witness to the Word of God. That says, *"No weapon formed against you will prosper,"* It cannot. **If God said that my son would get a new heart and live then he was going to get a new heart and live. The matter is settled in me and in Heaven.**

> "If God said that my son would get
> a new heart and live,
> then he was going to get
> a new heart and live.
> The matter is settled
> in me and in Heaven!"
> -
> ***Minister Liz Crockton***

Monday, February 24, 2014

Hospital
9:00am

Text message from Michael, his cousin, and my nephew:

"Liz, it's Michael. I am for the second time in my 46 years of life, I am terrified. I love Markel like my little brother I never had. We both have been through so much. He has helped me grow as a man, and I have helped him. It doesn't seem fair. He has never hurt anyone or done any harm. He is one of the outstanding guys. It pains me to see him going through all this. I will be there for him. You have always been like my second mom. You treated all of us like we are your own. It just isn't fair what we are going through at this moment. I know it will make us stronger, but how many tests can one family endure? I love you all. You know I NEVER should say this aloud or write it, ***but if there is a GOD, he needs to make this right.*** I know, I know…Don't get me wrong. I believe in something. Michael"

I have not responded to Michael. Someday, God will give me the word to comfort him. I know of his love for Markel and me. I know He knows what prayer can do. He was baptized and raised in the faith. I know he is angry with God for losing both of his parents. I know he is still hurting from having both of them die in his arms three years apart in the same hospital. I keep him covered in prayer knowing God can do a great thing in his life. I pray for his unbelief and the power of Markel's testimony of healing will speak to him about the power of God.

Marnier's testimony to her Dad (Markel's oldest daughter)

"Girls, I am sorry you have to see Dad looking like this."

"Looking like what, Dad," Marnier asked.

"Like this," he said, "weak and not able to take care of you girls and with half of my head missing."

She said, "Dad, even in your weakness, you are one of the strongest dads I know. In your weakness, God is still your strength. Lean on Him and lean on us too. Strength does not come from muscles and looks, Dad. Healing comes from your faith in God. That is what Grandma says. Have faith dad, Okay. You do look like a cartoon character–kind of cool."

The word of God says, **they that wait upon the Lord** *shall renew* **their** *strength;* **they** *shall mount up with wings as eagles;* **they** *shall run, and not be weary, and* **they** *shall walk, and not faint. (Isaiah 40:31)*

"Lord, help me to continue to put my trust in You and stand on Your word even when my present situation doesn't look like my Biblical Promise."

-

Markel Crockton

Friday, June 13, 2014

Hospital
The Operation to Replace Markel's Skull

Romans 8:28 – *And we know that for those who love God all things work together for good, for those who are called according to his purpose.*

We were called to the hospital two days before Father's Day to get Markel ready for surgery. He had to report early to stop the Coumadin- the blood thinner and get him started on a new medicine that was easier to finish before his surgery.

I said, "Why are they calling you two days before Father's Day? Couldn't the hospital wait until Monday and have you come in then? You have missed so many holidays with your girls, what would a few more days make?"

Markel said, "Mom, I am not sure, but we're going because I am tired of wearing this helmet and it's hot under here."

We arrived, and they started the treatment of taking him off Coumadin and started the new medication. The surgery was scheduled for Tuesday, June 17. The surgeon who had performed his first lifesaving surgery came to his room to see him. He told him about the procedure and asked if he had any questions. The doctors said the anesthesiologist and the team would be there later that night to get him ready for surgery the next morning. Early the following day, a group came to do some work and to get him prepared for surgery.

He was scheduled for surgery at 7:30am. He was told that there was a delay. At 11:45am, two nurses came and told us that the operation was not going to happen because they did not have an infusion person, and that the surgery would take place on Wednesday or Thursday, but they were not sure. On the following Wednesday around 3:30 pm, three people came into the room and told us that they were sorry but his bone specimen, namely his skull, was lost or thrown out by mistake.

But God Said...

Immediately, they had to take him down to get a CT scan to obtain images of his skull in order to make a prosthesis to replace his skull.

At 7:30pm, his doctor of neurology came and asked him to consider a cadaver bone to make his prosthesis. I asked Markel to weigh the pros and cons. Since Markel was on the heart transplant list, any changes or any new DNA or substance could alter things for his transplant. He had already gone through so much.

The surgeon was very upset that he had not been informed that his bone specimen was missing. He did not know how such a thing could happen hours before the surgery.

"I would like to know also," I said. "I do not understand how you could have a million-dollar team standing by an operation room reserved, and no one knew." My nerves were all over the place anticipating the surgery, and now this. Markel was as cool and calm as still water.

The doctor said that they would speed up the process to get the prosthesis made.

However, it would take a little over a week. The entire process that would typically take up to three months would be expedited and done in seven days. They could not send him home and wait because of the medication they had started on him that replaced the Coumadin. Now, he had to stay in the hospital because it would be more harmful to start and stop him on this medication than put him back on Coumadin. His surgeon was so upset, and he asked Mark, "How do you feel about all of this?"

Markel looked up and said, "It is incredible that all this is happening, but I want to know what happened, and why things weren't checked before I arrived." The doctor assured us that they would be looking into the whole situation and get back to us.

Markel stopped and looked at the doctor and said jokingly, "Are you sure some little old lady is not walking around with my skull growing an afro? Seriously, I believe God did not want me to have my old skull back after three months in the bone bank. It could have become diseased or something. What if you had put it into my head not knowing it was infected? That would have been a whole new set of issues. I am just going to trust God's plan on this one and move on."

One of the nurses told him, "Markel, you sure are taking this better than I would have. I do not think I could be that understanding if I were in your shoes."

A week and a half later, Markel went to surgery and things went well–praise God.

The funny thing was that the day that he was going to surgery, they had to send someone to Rhode Island to pick up the prosthesis. The prosthesis arrived a couple of hours before the operation.

I included this incident in this book because Markel said that God does not make mistakes, and there was a bigger plan in all of this for his life.

> "Whatever battle you are facing, remember, the war has already been won, the victory declared, Satan defeated, and God reign Supreme."
>
> **Markel Crockton**

But God Said...

Tuesday, February 25, 2014

Hospital
2:30am

I received a revelation from the Lord saying, write down what you have been asking me concerning your son. I wrote:

1. *Healing of Markel's own heart according to Your will*
2. *Healing of all seen and unseen neurological issues from the brain surgery*
3. *Heal him from all or any future blood clotting*
4. *All organs heal and not damaged by any medication or medical procedures*
5. *Healing of any his memory issues or nerve pains*
6. *He will live a long and full life according to Your promise*
7. *He will be restored to full health*
8. *Everything that the devil has tried to rob from him will be restored abundantly*
9. *He will give a testimony of praise talking about Your goodness, Your mercy, and Your healing power and would touch the lives of others so that they too will draw closer to you and will experience the power of Your might*
10. *All the devices in his body right now will not cause him harm, and they will work as designed*
11. *No infections will invade his body from those devices nor anything in the hospital*
12. *No viruses in his blood or in any parts of his body*
13. *His eyes are healed*

14. *His faith will grow stronger*

15. *His prayer life will become stronger*

16. *You will raise up new friends for him who will stick closer to him than brothers*

17. *He will have seasons of peace, excellent health, and prosperity*

It was revealed nothing else needed to be added to the list. I am sure that, in time, God will reveal why he wanted me to write this list for what I was believing Him to do.. I will wait for his revelation.

> "The Revelation of Jesus Christ, which God gave unto him, to shew unto his servants things which must shortly come to pass; and he sent and signified it by his angel unto his servant John:"
>
> **Revelation 1:1**

Wednesday, March 5, 2014

Hospital
6:30pm

Prayer time:

Father God, we bless Your name this day. We give You the glory, the honor, and the praise. Forgive us of our sins and have mercy on us this day.

You know the struggles and burdens we are facing as a family. Quiet our hearts and minds from any fears of sickness and uncertainties of life. Help us to stand by Your Word. Grant us the faith of a mustard seed that will grow in our lives to move mountains. Grant us Your peace and the authority from Your promised Word to speak to any personal storm that may be raging in life to cease. Set us free from pain, hurts, disappointments, broken promises, and raising dreams.

Help us to continue to put our trust in You and stand by Your Word even when our present situation does not look like our Biblical promise. Lord, continue to teach us to see what we still do not understand with the natural eyes. Lord, help us to hear what has not yet been spoken. Help us to stand guard and be on the watch when there is nothing visible to see or guard. Amen!

October 1, 2014

Hospital
9:00am

Today... bittersweet... Markel is getting a new heart today. As I rejoice, another mother is weeping over the loss of her son.

Father God, I thank You for everything. Please bring comfort and blessings to the family making this gift of life possible for my son. In Jesus Name!

> "Thank you, Lord, for Your keeping power. I am grateful that You did not allow the fires of life to consume me. The raging storms to destroy me, and sickness to take permanent resident in me."
>
> \- *Markel Crockton*

Conclusion

Living in Gratitude

"It is only with gratitude that life becomes rich!" – Dietrich Bonhoeffer

Due to the generosity of Markel's donor and God's grace, Markel has celebrated two birthdays: January 7th and October 1st. January 7th is his natural birthday, and October 1st is his second birthday and his second chance at life.

Markel has made a commitment to live his life with a heart of gratitude, knowing that his life is like a vapor. James 4:14 says, *"Yet you do not know what tomorrow will bring. For you are like a vapor that appears for a little time and then vanishes away."* He knows that his life is in God's hands and does not take it for granted. Therefore, he works in concert with his team of doctors by taking his life-saving medication religiously that keeps his new heart from rejection. He continues to keep the faith through prayer and stands on the Word of God.

Markel knows that everyone waiting for a heart transplant will not get the blessing he has received. Therefore, he tries to live a life that matters and pleases God. John Wesley said, " Do all the good you can, by all the means you can, in all the ways you can, in all the places you can, at all the time you can, to all the people you can, as long as ever you can." Markel embodies this saying by Wesley.

Although his donor's life was cut short, his heart lives on and has traveled to many places. Markel has traveled to family reunions, high school and college graduations, vacations, international cruises, high school proms, and accompanied his daughters to college. He also attends church, participate in various ministries and activities that help others.

"But God Said," his first book with his mother, is his testimony that miracles still happen, God answers prayer, there is power in prayer, and there is power in God's Word.

> **PRAYER**
> *Prayer is getting down on your knees, "before the only true and wise God," in total submission, surrendering your will to His will, and being in perfect peace even if His will to your prayer is not aligned to your expectation.*
> *-*
> *Minister Liz Crockton*

A Call for Action

If you are not an organ donor, please consider becoming a donor and encourage just one person in your village or family to do the same.

According to statistics, over 100,000 men, women, and children are on the national transplant waiting list and people die each day waiting for an organ transplant.

President Barack Obama said, "The decision to become a donor can save up to eight lives and enhance many more-men, women, and children who depend on the generosity and sacrifice of others. I encourage individuals of all ages and background to consider this unique opportunity to help those in need and to discuss this choice with family and friends."

Four Types of Donation
Living
Deceased
Tissue
Pediatric

Organ Donor Registries
Be The Match - www.bethematch.org
Donate Life - www.registerme.org
National Donate Life Registry - www.donatelife.net